In Search of the

Jacosaurus Costaricus

The Archosaur Inhalation Theorem based on evidences found of off the Pacific coast of Jaco Costa Rica

By

Rev. Nathon Q, Dees

Texas Guitar Legend

One day I was walking down the beach and a strange white stone caught my eye. After having taken an asswhooping trying to prove my meteorite find, I was not too excited about discovering more meteorites or dinosaur teeth because people are too stupid to understand you or see what you see. So I blew it off and walked on. Being brilliant can be a heavy burden sometimes.

So they went away and months later I was in deep meditation on Jaco beach and without even thinking about them the voice of my Higher self said,

"Sacred Geometry, rocks aren't formed in three".

I opened my eyes, stood up, and randomly selected six of the unique triangular forms that were all shaped like Texas and were the same color weight and consistency. They all showed intelligent design. The all were three sided, flat backed, and tapered with a socket root stem. They were as hard as ceramic and virtually erosion resistant. They showed no stratus or indication of being sedimentary stone or shellfish of any form. They were Petrified Archosaur teeth from the Triassic period.

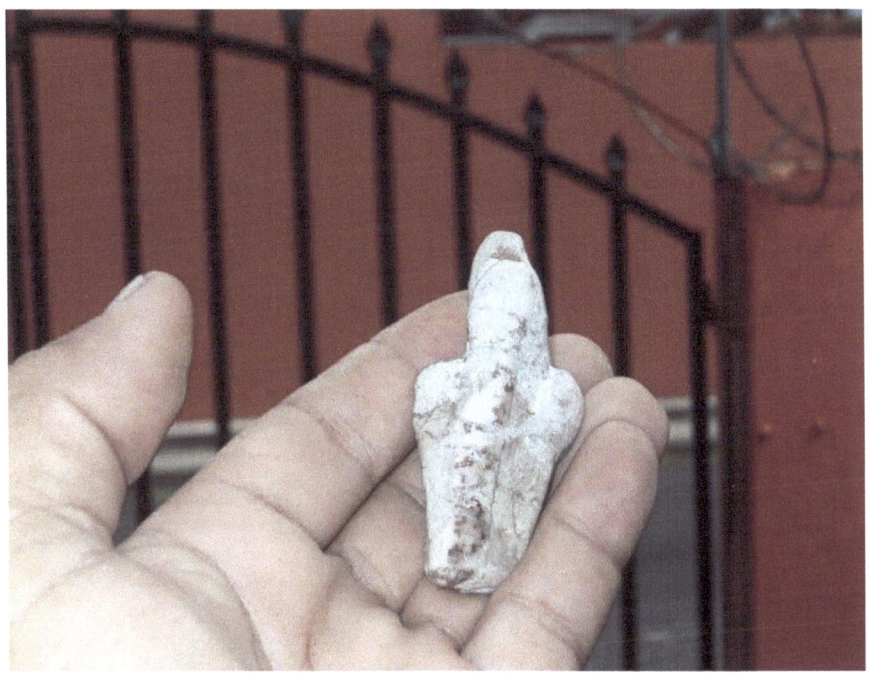

The Story Begins

In the mist of a primeval Triassic Tropic there once roamed the Mighty Jacosauros Costaricus. In the DNA metamorphosis that had been occurring during this period around 250 million years ago, there was one specific form of amphibious reptilian that had developed Thecodent socketed teeth. The majority of the Archosaurmorpha were destroyed in a major extinction event.

I propose that, off of the shore of Jaco Costa Rica on a low lying sea shelf there was once a low lying lake bed during the Pangaea era. This is where the mighty Jacosaurs roamed.

What in the Heck

Is a Jacosuar

Jacosaurs were Crocomorphus Gigantus that had triangular tapered socketed teeth that consisted of a cementem root base and dental stem cell that constantly replaced their teeth.

What is somewhat exclusive to the Jaosauar is its unique tapered triangular teeth. In researching fossil remains for a match of the form that I was finding, none of the traditional tooth fossils of the more popular dinosaurs or mammals were the same. There were certainly evidences of pre historic aquatic life forms predating the Megalodon and some forms of Pacicetus teeth and primitive aquatic mammalian, but what struck me the most were these very large triangular petrified teeth that I kept finding that I could not match to existing fossil records available to me.

They were large and powerful teeth designed to cut and tear. They literally fit together like a modern day cross cut seriated saw blade. A flat backside with a tapered triangular dentine that grew upward from a point at a large root base that went up into the gum line. The size and shape of its teeth made it one of the most efficient killing machines ever, on the land or in the water. Some that I have found are as small as ½ an inch while others are as much as 10 inches and weigh several pounds.

The fossil below still has the root coming out of the back of the tooth, It is visible to the upper right of the specimen proving my theory.

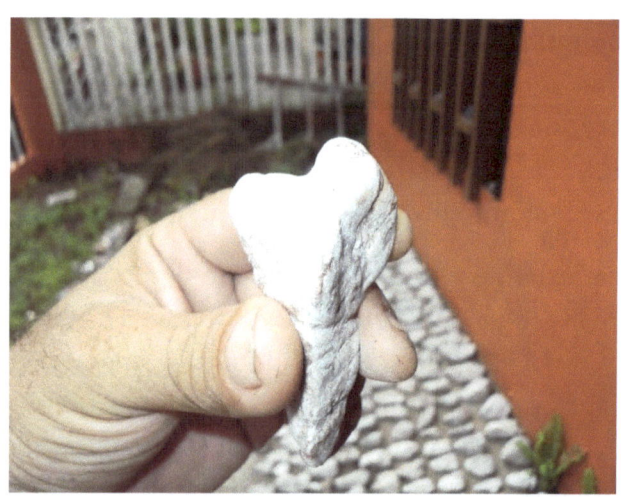

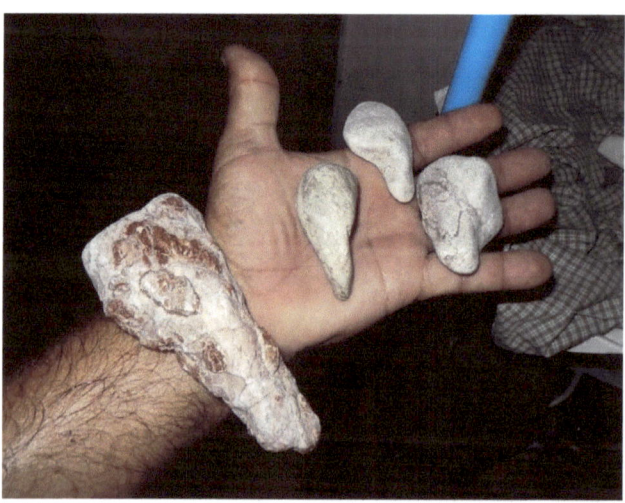

Archosauromorpha

Archosauromorpha (Greekfor "ruling lizard forms") is an infraclass of diapsid reptilesthat first appeared during the late Permian and became more common during the Triassic. It was defined by Jacques Gauthier, Arnold G. Kluge and Timothy Rowe (1988) as the group containing "archosaurs[i.e. Crocodylia, dinosaurs,birds, and several extinct orders] and all other sauriansthat are closer to archosaurs (s.s.) than they are tolepidosaurs (s.s.)" [i.e.tuataras, lizards, andsnakes]. In a later publication, Michel Laurin (1991) defined Archosauromorpha as theclade containing the most recent common ancestor ofProlacerta, *Trilophosaurus,Hyperodapedon* and archosaurs and all its descendants; David Dilkes (1998) formulated a more inclusive definition of Archosauromorpha, defining it as the clade containing*Protorosaurus* and all other saurians that are more closely related to*Protorosaurus* than to Lepidosauria.

Included in this infraclass are the groups Rhynchosauria, Trilophosauridae,Prolacertiformes and Archosauriformes. While superficially these reptiles vary in appearance (at one time they were even included in different subclasses – the trilophosaurs were considered euryapsids and the rhynchosaurs were considered lepidosaurs and were included in the same order as the tuatara), they are actually united by a number of small skeletal and skull-related details that suggest they form a clade that descended from a single common ancestor. Additional groups with uncertain phylogenetic position that are included in Archosauromorpha by some authors (and excluded from it by others) are Choristodera, drepanosaurs, thalattosaurs,ichthyopterygians, sauropterygians and turtles.

Of the taxa mentioned above, rhychosaurs, trilophosaurs and prolacertiforms died out at or before the end-Triassic extinction. The choristoderans continued as a minor group until the Miocene, and the Archosauriformes were important factors in early Triassic environments before giving rise to the even more successful Archosauria.

The Permian–Triassic (P–Tr) extinction event, one of several events colloquially known as the great dying, occurred about 252 <u>Ma</u> (million years) ago, forming the boundary between the <u>Permian</u> and <u>Triassic</u> <u>geologic periods</u>, as well as the <u>Paleozoic</u> and <u>Mesozoic</u> eras. It is the Earth's most severe known <u>extinction event</u>, with up to 96% of all <u>marine</u> <u>species</u> and 70% of <u>terrestrial</u> <u>vertebrate</u> species becoming <u>extinct</u>. It is the only known mass extinction of <u>insects</u>. Some 57% of all families and 83% of all genera became extinct. Because so much biodiversity was lost, the recovery of life on Earth took significantly longer than after any other extinction event, possibly up to 10 million years.

Researchers have variously suggested that there were from one to three distinct pulses, or phases, of extinction. There are several proposed mechanisms for the extinctions; the earlier phase was probably due to gradual environmental change, while the latter phase has been argued to be due to a catastrophic event. Suggested mechanisms for the latter include one or more large bolide impact events, massive volcanism, coal/gas fires and explosions from the Siberian Traps, and a runaway greenhouse effect triggered by sudden release of methane from the sea floor due to methane clathrate dissociation or methane-producing microbes; possible contributing gradual changes include sea-level change, increasing anoxia, increasing aridity, and a shift in ocean circulation driven by climate change.

In geology, petrifaction orpetrification is the process by which organic material is converted into stone through the replacement of the original material and the filling of the original pore spaces with minerals. Petrified wood is a common result of this process, but all organisms, from bacteria to vertebrates, can be petrified. Petrification takes place through a combination of two similar processes: permineralization and replacement. These processes create replicas of the original specimen that are similar down to the microscopic level.

Permineralization

One of the processes involved in petrification is permineralization. The fossils created through this process tend to contain a large amount of the original material of the specimen. This process occurs when groundwater containing dissolved minerals (most commonly <u>quartz</u>, <u>calcite</u>, <u>pyrite</u>, <u>siderite</u>(iron carbonate), and <u>apatite</u> (calcium phosphate)), fills pore spaces and cavities of specimens, particularly bone, shell or wood. The pores of the organisms' tissues are filled when these minerals precipitate out of the water. Two common types of permineralization are silicification and pyritization.

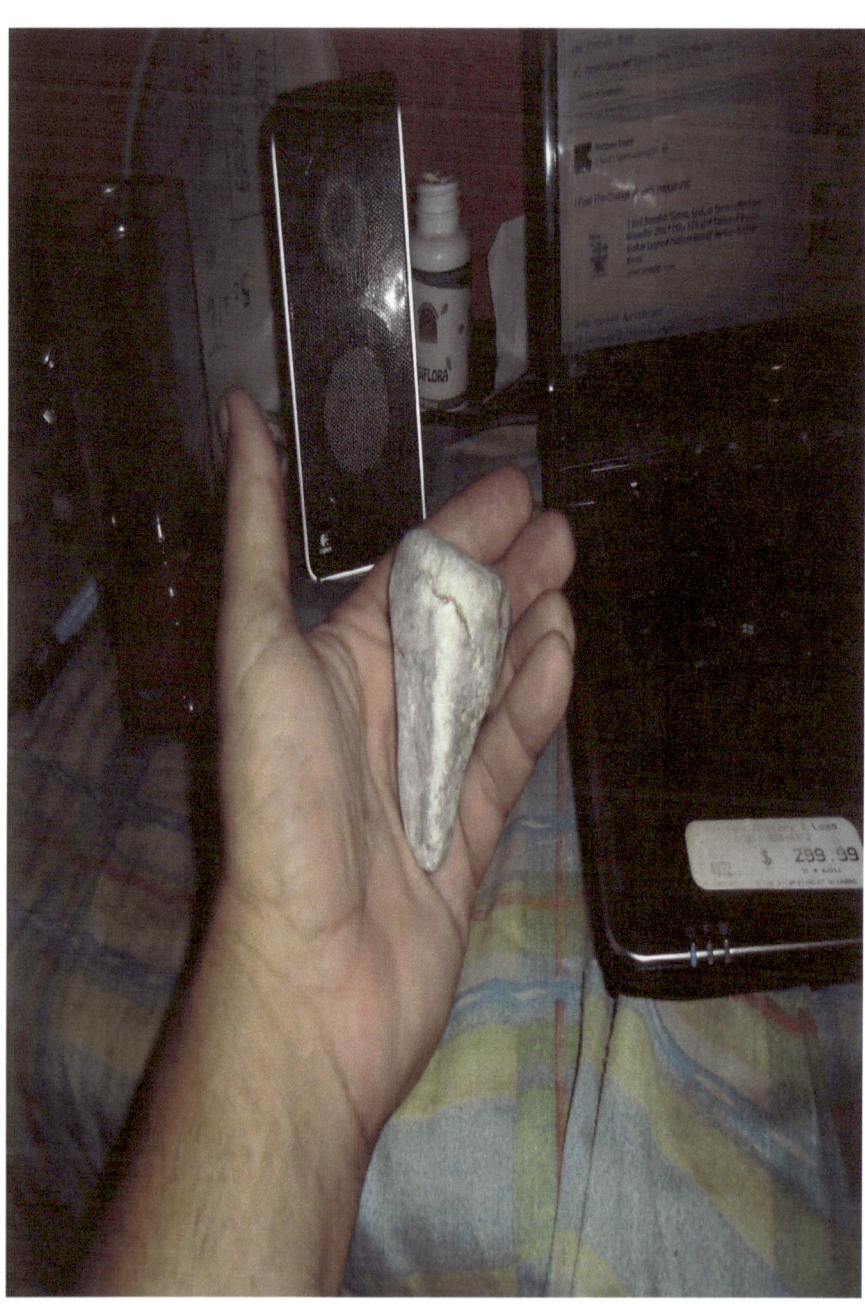

Anyone can plainly see the reoccurring triangular patterns in the petrified teeth. A strange new morph between a Megaloldon tooth and a Thecodent Crocomorphic Reptilian.

I have theorized by the consistency of the natural dentine color and nearly perfect tooth form in spite of the sea's erosion, that the Jacosaurs were more or less evaporated and the tooth pulp, root stems and dentem tooth base were petrified through molecular perminization and turned into a super hard ceramic calcite crystalline.

The three pictures above represent some of the different types of the flat backed triangular teeth in their many different forms and sizes. The second photo represents a prime specimen of one of the triangular Archosaur teeth that identify the species. The third photo shows some smaller teeth mounted from my private jewelry collection with some of the meteorites that I discovered from Texas.

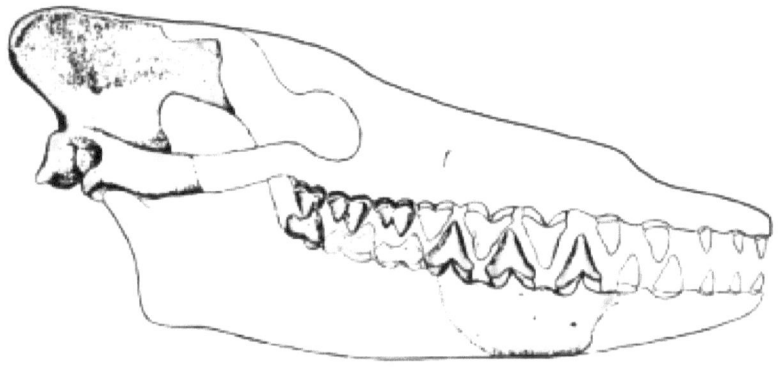

This Pakicetus was the first creature that showed the transition in tooth design and hunting and feeding challenges changed. You can see the combination of both tradition sea mammal teeth and the round more crocodile or gar like teeth in the front. The identification of this transition alone narrowed down both, the era, species and demise.

 This mass extinction during a massive evolutionary period
is the reason that this particular form petrified fossilized
teeth are such a rarity and have never been discovered
elsewhere in the world to my knowledge and all available
information on the Internet.

This is a prehistoric crocodile photo that I used without permission. You can see how that the massive teeth fit together perfectly in such a way as to rip, tear and cut. It is also noticeable how that the teeth are more triangular than round, like a more modern crocodile.

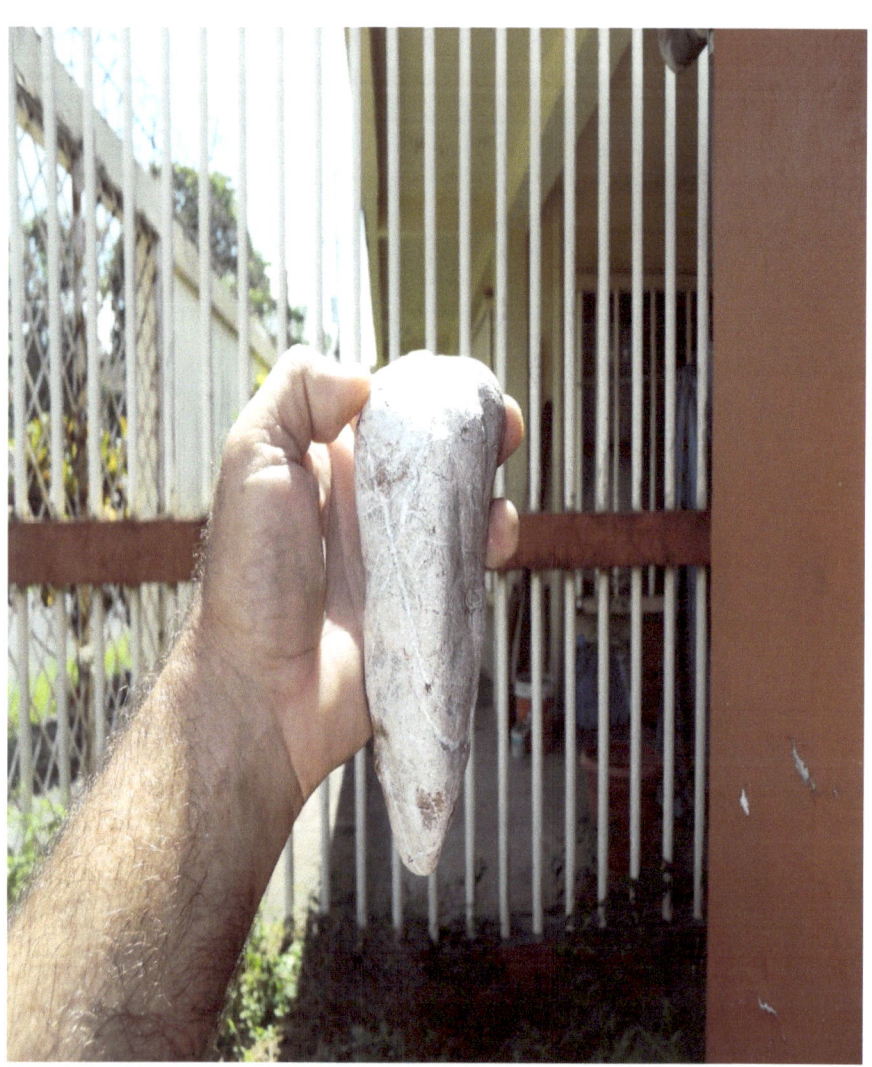

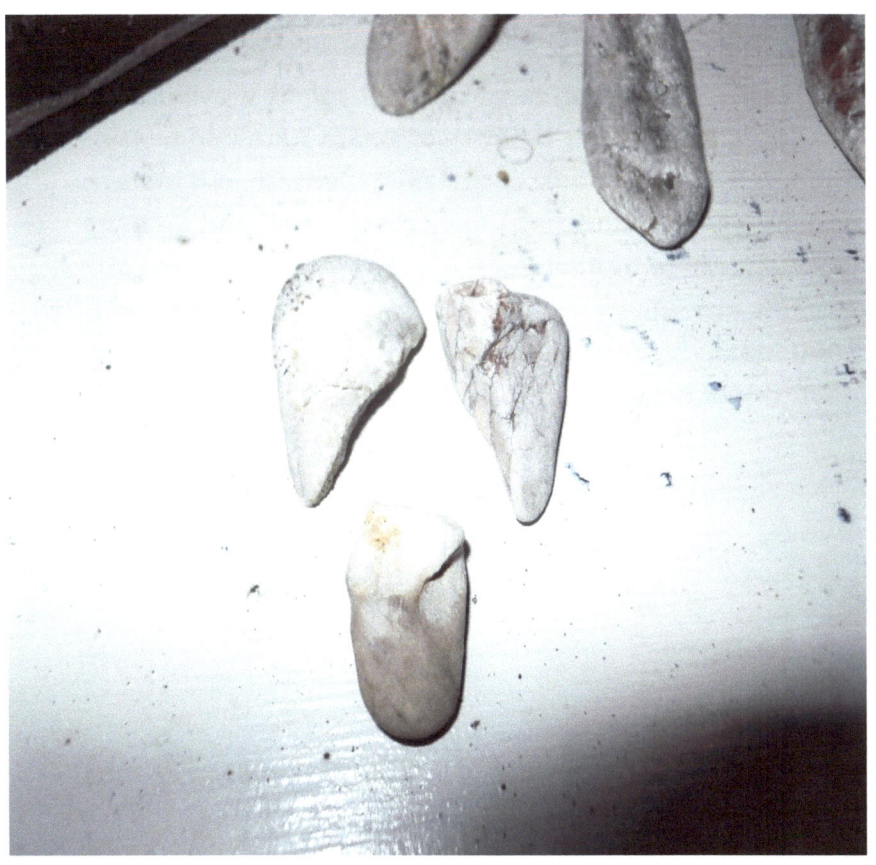

The information provided here was used without consent or permission from Wikipedia as where any photos other than my own.

This brief writing is an attempt to not only validate my historical find for the Country of Costa Rica and my town of Jaco, but also to reach out to the scientific and historic community to take what I have discovered and do a more in depth investigation and see just how many species of animals are represented in my Jacosaur collection of over 3000 fossils unique to any other place in the world than Jaco Costa Rica.

Thank you and Have a Nice Day

Rev Nathon Quinn Dees Jedi Master

Bonus Book Part 2

The Discovery

Of The

Deesite Textite

Stony Iron Metachondrite

Goethite Tektite/Meteorite

By Nathon Dees

One day I was sitting at my desk meditating and conversing with my higher self when I posed myself this question " How in the Fuck am I supposed to fund an enlightenment movement and fulfill the destiny that you have shown me with no fucking cash man?".

To which the voice of reason resounded "What is the stupidest thing that you could do to get money Son?" and I said "God pick up a stupid fucking rock worth Millions of dollars". Then the voice responded with another question "What do Templars do?". Look for treasure? "Then get up off your ass and start looking for treasure dumbass!". So I did.

I started looking at the geology of the land around me and was aware of some of the elements present in the area so I started prospecting for placer gold. After finding small amounts of place gold I of course went deeper into the creek bed into its lowest points where the heaviest minerals are deposited.

Everything was Texas Limestone. Ten foot high walls of nothing but limestone, Quartz and Dolomite shelves along the sides of the creek bed like a small perdenal. While looking in the crevices of the Blue stone creek bed I heard the voice say "Find the Ore, Find the Gold". To which I naturally responded "There's no

Fucking ore here man there's nothing but,,,
What the hell is that?".

Abstract

The surface of the Earth has been bombarded continually by meteorites since it first accreted 4 6 billion years ago, Texas' relative tectonic stability and prolonged aridity has provided an ideal site for the accumulation of meteorites over a long period of time, The Edward's Plateau and the Texas hill country has been the host to many meteorites as well as East Texas and the gulf Coast. The strewn field in Question is located in northern Hays County Texas and runs parallel to the Bediasite Tektite strewn field.

 I had personally found over 150lbs of a brown carbonoid cryptocrystalline Diamagnetic Iron Goethite specimens that ranged in size from one gram to five pounds. The mineral deposits were clearly identifiable to the trained eye as Texas Stony Iron meteorites.

These are pictures of **100% AUTHENTIC Stony Iron Chondrite Meteorites from city of West, Texas area." That are on E bay and other online stores.**

1mm

10mm

25mm

46 Chondrite Meteorites
Aprox: 50 grams

They were a brownish rust color but not rusted or eroded in any way. They had the frozen flight and splash shapes that are common with Australian Tektites IE Rollers, buttons, tear drops,dumb bells, and balls.

They are Diamagnetic and magnetically Oppose other samples of Deesite Textite and quartz from all sides like an Orgone dissimilar polar reaction. They are non conductive and withstand temperatures in excess of 2,000f without melting. Most of all they had both Fusion Crust and Regmaglyphs. Not only did they have fusion crust it was clearly heat intensive in its coloration to the weighted in flight sides of the ores.

As meteoroids are heated during atmospheric entry, their surfaces melt and experience ablation. They can be sculpted into various shapes during this process, sometimes resulting in deep "thumb-print" like indentations on their surfaces called regmaglypts. If the meteoroid maintains a fixed orientation for some time, without tumbling, it may develop a conical "nose cone" or "heat shield" shape. As it decelerates, eventually the molten surface layer solidifies into a thin fusion crust, which on most meteorites is black (on some achondrites, the fusion crust may be very light colored).

On stony meteorites, the heat-affected zone is at most a few mm deep; in iron meteorites, which are more thermally conductive, the structure of the metal may be affected by heat up to 1 centimetre (0.39 in) below the surface. Reports vary; some meteorites are reported to be "burning hot to the touch" upon landing, while others have been cold enough to condense water and form a frost.[12][13][14] Meteorites from multiple falls such as Bjurbole, Tagish Lake, and Buzzard Coulee have been found having fallen upon lake and sea ice, perhaps suggesting that they were not hot when they fell.

Meteoroids that experience disruption in the atmosphere may fall as meteorite showers, which can range from only a few up to thousands of separate individuals. The area over which a meteorite shower falls is known as its strewn field. Strewn fields are commonly elliptical in shape, with the major axis parallel to the direction of flight. In most cases, the largest meteorites in a shower are found farthest down-range in the strewn field.

Most of all, there is no naturally occurring Goethite or Limonite in Northern Hays County. There is only Limestone, Quartz, and Dolomite. There are no ancient Volcanoes, Mines, Mills, Railroads, Forges, bog ores or any reason for Iron Meta Ore Nodules strewn over a specific area over nothing but ancient limestone sea beds.

I personally have over 30 years of experience working in Hays County as a professional Builder and Licensed Texas Aerobic Waste Water Specialist OFFS2 and it is my professional opinion that the Goethite ore in question is not any form of Native Central Texas stone that can be found in Hays County Texas other than the strewn field in Question. It is in fact non Terrestrial in Origin and at the absolute least a Tektite.

Photos of the Deesite Textite

My friend's company Cerium Labs and Leica Instruments hosted a symposium. After the talks, He played on the awesome Leica light microscopes. Here are a few pictures

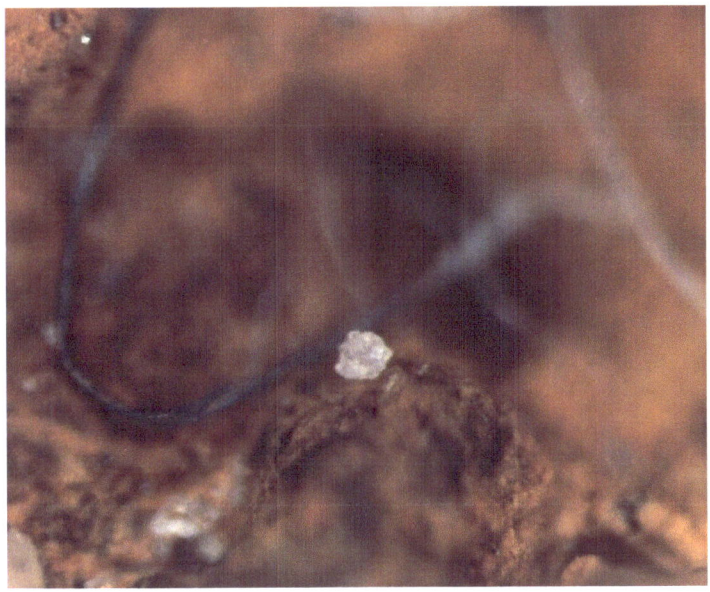

You will notice that there are obvious regmaglyphs on the surface of the stones featured bellow. There are no outward bubbling formations as found in bog Ore or Goethite Limonite in their natural forms.

Anyone one can see the many common meteorite and Tektite forms represented in this photo but most impressive are the in flight perminalization and the multi colored fusion crust that can only found on Meterites and Tektites.

This is the largest one weighing nearly 2.5 lbs. It was Given to the Houston
Museum of Natural Science by my friend Erra Lana Love for validation and
they refused to return it after countless attempts. They still have it.

53.8g
D13

72.6g
D14

65.6g
D15

54.7g
D16

56.0g
D17

61.7g
D18

58.6g
D19

47.3g
D20

Tektites *(from Greek τηκτός "tēktos", molten) are gravel-size bodies that are composed of black, green, brown or gray, natural glass that are formed from terrestrial debris ejected during extraterrestrial impacts. They are characterized by 1. a fairly homogeneous composition; 2. an extremely low content of water and other volatiles; 3. an abundant lechatelierite; 4. a general lack of microscopic crystals known as microlites and chemical relation to the local bedrock or localsediments; and 5. their distribution within geographically extensivestrewnfields. Tektites generally range in size from centimeters to millimeters. Millimeters-size tektites are known as microtektites.*

Although tektites are superficially similar to some terrestrial volcanic glasses (obsidians), they have unusual distinctive physical characteristics that distinguish them from such glasses. First, they are completely glassy and lack any microlites or phenocrysts unlike terrestrial volcanic glasses. Second, although high in silica (>65 wt%), the bulk chemical and isotopic composition of tektites is closer to those of shales and similar sedimentary rocks and quite different from the bulk chemical and isotopic composition of terrestrial volcanic glasses. Third, tektites contain virtually no water (<0.02 wt%) unlike terrestrial volcanic glasses. Fourth, the flow-banding within tektites often contains particles and bands of lechatelierite, which are not found in terrestrial volcanic glasses. Finally, a few tektites contain partly melted inclusions of shocked and unshocked mineral grains, i.e. quartz,apatite, and zircon, as well as coesite.

The difference in water content can be used to distinguish tektites from terrestrial volcanic glasses. When heated to their melting point, terrestrial volcanic glasses will turn into a foamy glass because of their content of water and other volatiles. Unlike terrestrial volcanic glass, a tektite will produce only a few bubbles at most when heated to its melting point because of its much lower water and other volatiles content.

On the basis of morphology and physical characteristics, tektites have traditionally been divided into four groups. The tektites which have been found on land have traditionally been subdivided into three groups: (1) splash-form (normal) tektites, (2) aerodynamically shaped tektites, and (3) Muong Nong-type (layered) tektites. Splash-form and aerodynamically shaped tektites are only differentiated on the basis of their appearance and some of their physical characteristics. Splash-form tektites are centimeter-sized tektites that are shaped like spheres, ellipsoids, teardrops, dumbbells, and other forms characteristic of isolated molten bodies. They are regarded as having formed from the solidification of rotating liquids, and not atmospheric ablation. Aerodynamically shaped tektites, which are mainly part of the Australasian strewn field, are splash-form tektites (buttons) which display a secondary ring or flange. The secondary ring or flange is argued as having been produced during the high-speed reentry and ablation of a solidified splash-form tektite into the atmosphere. Muong Nong tektites are typically larger, greater than 10 cm in size and 24 kg in weight, irregular, and layered tektites. They have a chunky, blocky appearance, exhibit a layered structure with abundant vesicles, and contain mineral inclusions, such as zircon, baddeleyite, chromite, rutile, corundum, cristobalite and coesite.

Bediasite is a form or type of tektite. It originates in an area in the eastern part of the U.S. state of Texas centered around the small town of Bedias which is 74 miles (119 km) north west of Houston.[1] They are found in about nine Texas Counties in an area of over 7,000 square miles (18,000 km^2). The largest specimen ever found is just over 200 grams.

Virgil Barnes was one of the first scientists to study Bediasites in depth. The first identified Bediasite was brought to the University of Texas at Austin in 1936 by George D. Ramsey and was identified by Virgil Barnes.[2]

Bediasites are part of the 34-million-year-old North American strewnfield coming from the Chesapeake Bay impact crater.[3] Two strewnfields and tektite groups are associated with this impact: the black Bediasites in Texas and the green Georgiaites in Georgia.[4]

The Deesite Textite strewn field is parallel to the Bediaste Strewn Field about forty miles to the West along the Edwards Escarpment South of Austin in Northern Hays County.

I propose that the Deesite Textite Is a form of new form of Tektite created from Molten Goethite being unearthed by a comet strike at the Gulf coast of Texas and that is in fact where the Bediasite was formed as well discounting the opinion of the Late Virgil Barns. I propose that both the bediasite Tektite and the Deesite Textite were created by a comet strike on the Gulf Coast shore of Texas. With my understanding of field artillery 13 Foxtrot in the U.S. Army I realize that it was preposterous for professor Barns to ever assume that the Bediasite could have possibly flown all the way from the East Coast at the Chesapeake Bay strike to Texas and land in a perfect strewn field with no evidence anywhere else between Georgia where the Georgiasite Tektite is found and from Houston to Austin where the Bediasite Tektite is found. Bothe the Bediasite Tektite and the Deesite Textite were formed from a Comet strike on the Texas Gulf Coast that melted the native minerals into hurling meteoroids/tektoids of molten earthen materials native to the Texas gulf Coast. This would account for its shape form, color, location, Goethite content and diamagnatsm. The only other valid explanation would be that they are in fact prehistoric Stony Iron Metachondrites and no one is willing to pay for the testing necessary to either validate or invalidate my theory.

---------- Forwarded message ----------
From Doug Nash
Date: Wed, Jul 9, 2014 at 7:39 PM
Subject: meteorites

That's the conclusion we draw from both hand specimen examination of the two stones, and especially their thin section exam under the microscopes here in Hawaii (see attached picture of one of the thin section views).

Two successful thin sections, one for each of the two stones. were made at the Univ. of Hawaii's Labidary Dept (JoAnn Sinton) and completed July 8, 2014, and examined same day under a modern petrographic microscope in the Petrology Lab at the Hawaii Institute for Geophysics and Planetary Science (by Dr. Jeff Taylor---- who I've known for years and is a highly recognized Meteorite Research scientist and planetary science Professor at U.H.).

Results revealed that the two stones are composed of fine-grained iron oxide minerals, best represented by the mineral Goethite, which chemically is an iron hydroxide mineral, typically represented by the formula $Fe^{3+}O(OH)$. It's a nonmagnetic, dark blackish-brown mineral material, that leaves a brown streak, and is fairly heavy, but less heavy than metallic iron. It is often mixed with Limonite, also an iron oxide mineral, plus others similar.

The thin sections indicate that there are no characteristics in the two stones you sent me suggesting that they are meteorites.

Further exam (beyond the thin sections) would be very complex and expensive and are not warranted for further testing for meteorites by what the thin sections have revealed.

My conclusion after considering these results, and discussing with my colleague Jeff Taylor (and reviewing pertinent online literature -- see addirional attachment) is that the stones you sent are simply iron rich, non-silicate, non-carbonate rocks, and most likely related to iron-bearing rocks widely known to occur in Texas and have been mined from various locations there for many years.

Doug Nash

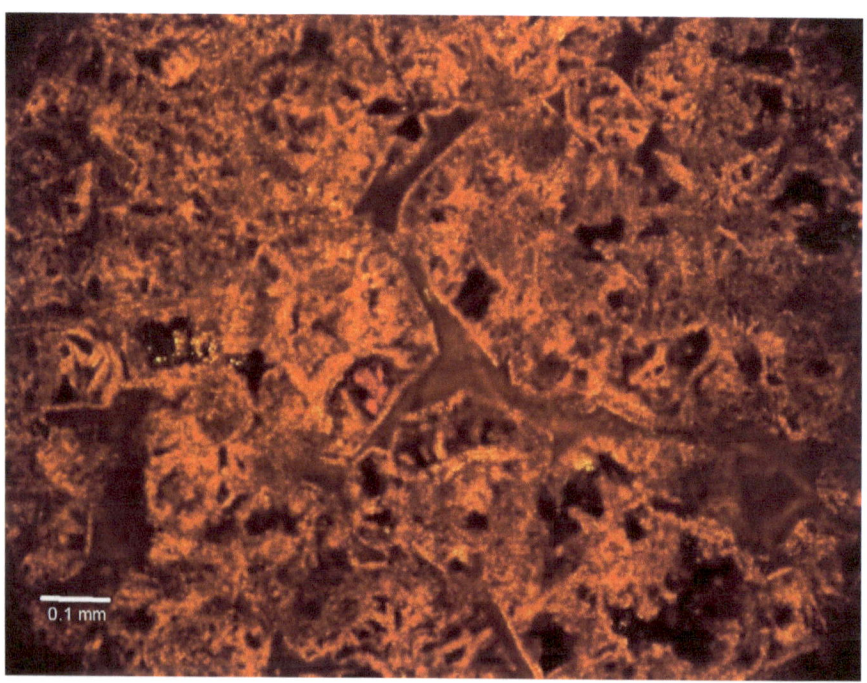

This is a petrographic slide of the Deesite Textite above Taken by Doug Nash who has worked with J.P.L. and N.A.S.A. Taken at the University of Hawaii.

This is a photo of native Texas Goethite which has absolutely no similarity whatsoever to the Deesite Textite although they share the same minerals. In fact no one can provide me with a single specimen of Goethite/Limonite on Earth that even remotely resembles the Deesite Textite in shape, color, or form.

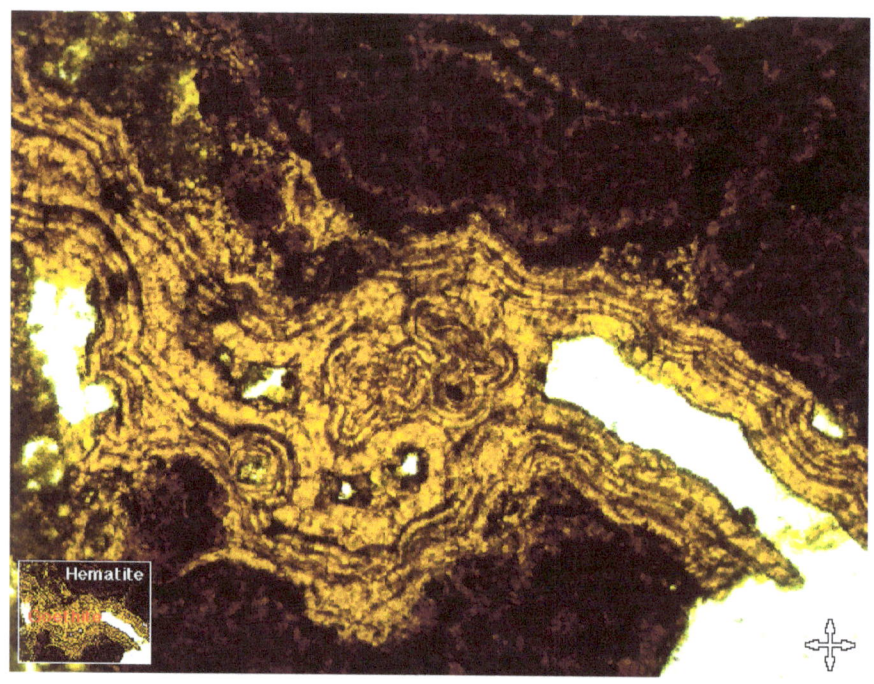

Goethite _ –Fe3+O(OH)

Crystal Data: Orthorhombic. *Point Group: 2/m2/m2/m.* As prismatic crystals, striated
k [001], to 45 cm, or tabular on {010}. More commonly as aggregates of capillary to acicular crystals, in divergent sprays, or reniform, botryoidal, or stalactitic masses with concentric or radial fibrous internal structure; nearly cryptocrystalline in "limonite".

Physical Properties: *Cleavage:* {010}, perfect; {100}, less perfect.
Fracture: Uneven.

Tenacity: Brittle. Hardness = 5–5.5 VHN = 667 (100 g load). D(meas.) = 4.28(1)
D(calc.) = 4.18

Optical Properties: Opaque, transparent on thin edges. *Color:* Blackish brown; yellowish
to reddish brown in massive aggregates, may be banded; shades of yellow in thin section; gray
with bluish tint in reflected light, with yellow, red, brown internal reflections.
Streak: Brownish
yellow, yellow-orange, ocher-yellow. *Luster:* Imperfect adamantine metallic to dull earthy; silky
when fibrous.
Chemistry: (1) (2)
SiO_2 0.36
Fe_2O_3 89.65 89.86
H_2O 10.19 10.14
Total 100.20 100.00
  (1) El Paso Co., Colorado, USA. (2) FeO(OH).
  (2) **Polymorphism & Series:** Trimorphous with feroxyhyte and
    lepidocrocite.
Occurrence: A common weathering product derived from numerous iron-bearing minerals in
oxygenated environments; an important component of ore in weathered iron deposits. Also a
primary precipitate in hydrothermal, marine, and bog environments upon oxidation of reduced
iron-bearing waters.
Association: Lepidocrocite, hematite, pyrite, siderite, pyrolusite, manganite, many other iron and
manganese-bearing species.
Distribution: Widespread

Name: Honors the German poet, dramatist, and philosopher, Johann Wolfgang von Goethe (1749–1832).
References: (1) Palache, C., H. Berman, and C. Frondel (1944) Dana's system of mineralogy, (7th edition), v. I, 680–687. (2) Deer, W.A., R.A. Howie, and J. Zussman (1962) Rock-forming minerals, v. 5, non-silicates, 118–121. (3) Harrison, R.K., N. Aitkenhead, B.R. Young, and P.F. Dagger (1975) Goethite from Hindlow, Derbyshire. Bull. Geol. Surv. Great Britain, 52, 51–54.
  (3) Ramdohr, P. (1980)

"Stone of Death & Rebirth"
Goethite helps attune to the ethereal.

Goethite, is a stone with frequencies vibrating powerful healing energies. This stone has many advantages when it comes assisting one with its metaphysical properties. However, one of it's most beneficial abilities is its potential to heal through grief by diving deep into the self to dig up wounds buried within the unconscious.

Goethite is a stone for discovering and then enhancing the soul life.
Goethite, also, has the ability to bring one into confrontation with the true core of their reality. This will result in the recovery of things once lost, along with the surfacing of repressed grief, which is a primal emotion poorly handled in modern society. Grief will bring tears and tears showcase a sign of healing.

Excellent for assisting walk-ins and inter-dimensionals in connecting to Earth's vibration
Goethite stimulates the emotional body within the etheric body. In return, one will become more consciously aware of the emotions throughout their entire spectrum. It help open the heart and awakens one to compassion and love.

Goethite is a powerful aid to artists, writers and musicians.
Goethite stimulates the mind to move into the stage of recognition, the need to face and sort through, and let go of any shadows of the self that are held within but locked away. Goethite helps in conquering the "shadow self" never to be heard or seen again. It also helps to see the "shadow self" in a positive light. It then leads into the stages of integrating and letting go to ascend into higher states of consciousness.

Encourages one to look within, face and conquer the "Shadow Self".

I'm just trying to get information across and reach some level of understanding here not get a Grade in English or science

. Thank You. Nathon Q, Dees

The End.

www.ingramcontent.com/pod-product-compliance
Lightning Source LLC
Chambersburg PA
CBHW050841290526
45792CB00001B/482